Heading Home Book

15 Simple Steps to a Successful Military Transition

Transitioning from military service back into civilian life is an exciting and challenging time.

In this Itty Bitty® Book, U.S. Navy veteran, Carolyn R. Owens, shows you simple strategies you can use to make the process much more enjoyable and reduce overwhelm and frustration.

Begin your transition process by following these simple, but important steps to chart your course and you will have an edge over the competition, allowing you to breathe a little easier.

For example:

- Begin the process earlier rather than later.
- Research potential job markets/leads.
- Don't underestimate using social media as a tool for networking, job search or promoting a business.
- How to effectively address adversities and setbacks to achieve success.

Pick up a copy of this powerful book today and develop a successful plan for the next phase of your career and life! But most of all, thank you for your service!

Your Amazing Itty Bitty® Heading Home Book

15 Simple Steps to a Successful Military Transition

Carolyn R. Owens

Published by Itty Bitty® Publishing
A subsidiary of S & P Productions, Inc.

Copyright © 2016 **Carolyn R. Owens**

All rights reserved. No part of this book may be reproduced or transmitted in any form or by any means, electronic or mechanical, including photocopying, recording or by any information storage and retrieval system, without written permission of the publisher, except for inclusion of brief quotations in a review.

Printed in the United States of America

Itty Bitty® Publishing
311 Main Street, Suite D
El Segundo, CA 90245
(310) 640-8885

ISBN: 978-1931191-1-80

This Itty Bitty Book is dedicated to all who have served, are currently serving and will serve, together with their families and friends who have supported them along their journey. I wish you all an easy and successful transition back to civilian life (CIVLANT)...

I also want to dedicate this book to my son, DeJuan, who enjoyed my journey with me – it was an adventure! Fairwinds and following seas...

Stop by our Itty Bitty® website to find interesting blog entries regarding career transitions and personal and professional development.

www.IttyBittyPublishing.com

or visit Carolyn R. Owens at:

www.infinitycoaching.net

cowens@infinitycoaching.net

Table of Contents

Introduction
- Step 1. Charting the Course – Start Early
- Step 2. Military Transition Programs
- Step 3. Nice to Meet YOU – Conduct a Self-Assessment
- Step 4. Research – Do Your Homework
- Step 5. Assess Your Skill Gaps
- Step 6. Make A Financial Plan
- Step 7. Network - Who Do You Know?
- Step 8. The Power of Social Media
- Step 9. LinkedIn - Virtual Networking
- Step 10. Get A Mentor
- Step 11. Writing Your Resume
- Step 12. The Roller Coaster Ride
- Step 13. Compensation and Benefits
- Step 14. Federal, Private or Non-Profit
- Step 15. Your Mindset

Introduction

In this book you will find 15 Itty Bitty steps you can take to make your transition easier and more enjoyable. This list does not encompass everything you need to know or do. It serves to highlight key steps, serving as a guide during this critical time.

During my 24+ years on active duty and, as a career strategist and leadership coach, I have assisted numerous service members with their transitions, learning, guiding and taking a lot of notes. I did the research, read the books and came up with a plan of action for my own very successful transition and have passed that knowledge on to many others. I have now summarized the key steps in this book. Steps that allowed me to retire stress and debt free. You can do the same thing!

The process will not always be easy, as this will be new terrain for you to cover, but hopefully this book will make the journey a little bit smoother.

Step 1
Charting the Course – Start Early

Transitioning from military service back into the civilian sector is an exciting and challenging time. In this Itty Bitty Book you will find 15 simple steps that will make the process much more enjoyable, reducing overwhelm and frustration. The key is to begin the process earlier, rather than later.

1. Start planning as early as two years before your pending separation or retirement.
2. Being proactive about the process will allow you to have all of your documentation in order.
3. Early planning allows for those being impacted by the transition to fully understand the process.
4. Planning ahead allows time for career exploration.
5. With advanced planning, you can make the process fun – a new adventure.

How to Chart the Course:

- Keep a transition notebook that includes ideas, timelines, points of contacts with names, addresses, phone numbers, schools and certifications.
- Have an accountability partner – someone you can meet with monthly or weekly that will ask the tough questions.
- Have a doctor review your medical history and summarize any/all medical issues throughout your career on a page at the front of your record/electronic file.
- Set the tone and have a positive attitude about the process.

Step 2
Military Transition Programs

Many service members will think they know everything about the transition process and therefore don't need to attend these courses. Not attending is a huge mistake – you can miss that one piece of information that you need to have a smooth transition. The programs are designed to better prepare you to transition from military to civilian life.

1. If your friends told you it was not valuable for them – ignore them! You still need to attend. Your experience will be different than theirs.
2. You will learn more information from the questions your classmates ask.
3. If you can, attend a course two years before separation/retirement and then another one year to six months before.
4. Have your transition notebook with you and take plenty of notes.
5. If you are on deployment and not able to attend at least once a year, ask if you can obtain a copy of the manuals given out during class.

Advantages to Attending a Transition Course:

- The information you receive can be used to develop your transition timeline in order to chart your course.
- Make new connections with your classmates; many of mine became connections on LinkedIn.
- Meet the instructors/presenters, some of whom are recruiters or Human Resource professionals, who will take time to look at your resume and provide other valuable advice.
- Get the latest updates on programs and benefits.
- Learn who to go to when you need assistance. I met a representative from the Veterans of Foreign Wars (VFW), http://www.vfw.org/, who assisted me with the Disability Benefit claim; his help expedited the claim process.

Step 3
Nice to Meet YOU –
Conduct a Self-Assessment

It's time to take an honest look at YOU. Spend time reflecting over your career and the time before you came in the military. Spend time learning about yourself – what motivates and drives you.

1. Schedule time where you can be in a relaxed environment, undisturbed and think about what your purpose is. Keep in mind this is what YOU want, not what someone else wants.
2. Conduct an internet search of career assessments to find questions that will help you.
3. Conduct online personality assessments.
4. Review your career history.
5. Ask friends, family and colleagues for their views on what you'd be good at.
6. You do not have to accomplish this all at once, you should schedule several times allowing for review and reflection of your notes.
7. Be sure to write the answers down in your notebook, as you will need to review them when you develop your roadmap.

Some Questions to Ask YOURself:

- What did you enjoy most about your career?
- What are your strengths, weaknesses and skills?
- What do you really like to do?
- Take time to review the skills, education and certifications you have acquired and earned.
- What kind of work are you interested in doing?
- Take a personality assessment that is effective in giving you a general idea of your talents and abilities and assists you with identifying the type of career you truly want, such as Energy Leadership Index (ELI) Assessment, DISC or the Myers Briggs Type Indicator (MBTI).
- For more support and guidance, hire a career coach or counselor.

Step 4
Research – Do Your Homework

Now that you have spent time conducting a self-assessment, you have a few ideas on what you consider as an ideal job. The next step will be to research some potential job markets/leads.

1. The internet is the MOST powerful research tool available today.
2. You can find information on the industry, position, companies, salary, etc. that interest you – all at the push of a few computer keys.
3. If you know someone who is currently or has been in a position you are interested in, give them a call. People love to talk about what they know and do.
4. Review job leads and jobs that interest you, then find what you consider a good job, and what you need to do to get there.

Things to Consider When Conducting Research:

Look at various job sites and study the announcements. What type of language/keywords are they using? Make note of the knowledge, skills and experience required.

- Develop a list of potential employers.
- Consider Federal, Non-Profit and Private sector organizations (See Step 14).
- Does the company mission align with your personal mission and values?
- Some of the popular sites on which you can review announcements and develop a potential list of employers are:
    - http://www.indeed.com
    - http://www.simplyhired.com
    - https://www.theladders.com
    - https://www.usajobs.gov
    - https://www.glassdoor.com
    - http://www.monster.com

Step 5
Assess Your Skill Gaps

Spend time going through the data you collected, comparing the information with your knowledge, skills and experience.

1. Did you identify any skills that you were missing? If so, are you willing to go back to school to acquire the certification or degree required?
2. Your employment prospects may improve if you get some additional education and training. Plus, you may be able to do so before you leave the military. Many graduate schools have evening programs to accommodate working adults.
3. Leading universities now offer online programs you can take anywhere. Consider internships to get additional skills, or volunteer for a position in the field.

What if You Don't Have All the Skills Needed?

- Consider taking an internship. This is a great way to get your foot in the door.
- Obtain a certification or attend a trade program. Spend time searching for free programs/classes offered by some states.
- Look at similar jobs in the career field/industry you are interested in. You may be able to take a different position to get your foot in the door or gain the experience you need.

- After taking a hard look at the announcements, salary, etc. you may realize you want to consider a whole different industry. If so, conduct some additional research on areas that had piqued your interest during your self-assessment.

Step 6
Make a Financial Plan

Financial Planning is often one of the steps that is overlooked when transitioning; however it can impact the flexibility you have in making decisions.

1. Make sure you create a financial plan that includes a budget listing ALL of your current expenses.
2. Start by asking what will change once you leave the military.
3. Estimate what your retirement pay will be and remember to include items such as medical, dental and housing expenses you are not accustomed to paying.
4. Try tracking your spending for 30 days and see where your money is really going; you might be surprised.
5. Most importantly, start saving money and work to become debt-free before you leave the service. Choosing to save will give you more control over your career path.

Key things to Consider When Creating a Financial Plan:

- If you don't have a budget, create one.
- Consider what expenses you won't have when you retire/separate from service.
- Know what assets you have. Many people can't even tell you what is in their savings and investment accounts.
- Have you been robbing Peter to pay Paul? In other words, using credit cards to pay regular bills?
- Try to be able to pay expenses for a minimum of three months, but if possible, longer.
- Are there any debts that need to be paid to the government before separation/retirement, such as advanced pay or overpayments?
- Meet with a financial planner. The United Services Automobile Association (USAA), Military Officers Association of America (MOAA) and your credit union all offer these services.
- Have your will drafted or updated.

- For some careers, employers may want to obtain a copy of your credit report. This is legal, as long as they ask you first. Get a copy before you start the interview process so you can be prepared to address any discrepancies.

Step 7
Network

"The richest people in the world look for and build networks. Everyone else looks for work." Robert Kiyosaki

Effective networking is still the number one way people find out about jobs and secure a position. Most people are uncomfortable with networking or don't know how to network effectively. What you may not realize is that you do have some experience networking. Think about all of the mandatory social events you had to attend and the times you volunteered in the community. That was networking!

1. Networking is about making connections and building relationships.
2. Your local chamber of commerce is a great resource to research local groups and events.
3. **If** you are using networking as part of your job campaign, don't ask for a job right away; establish a rapport/ relationship first.

Strategies for Effective Networking:

- Practice talking about what you do so you appear confident and won't stumble over your words.
- Do you have business or calling cards to share, if asked? If not, have some made. On the front, at a minimum include your full name, email address and phone number. On the back, include key words so they will remember what areas you specialize in.
- Write down key information on any business cards you receive so you don't forget why you want to follow up with someone.
- Join associations that are relevant to the industry you are interested in. A great site that lists associations is: http://weddles.com/associations
- Great books to read on networking -
    - *Perfect Pairings: The Art of Connecting People* by Jessica Levin
    - *How to Be a Power Connector* by Judy Robinett
    - *Never Eat Alone* by Keith Ferrazzi

Step 8
The Power of Social Media

Don't underestimate using social media as a tool for networking, job search or promoting a business you may start. Many employers now advertise positions and look for candidates on social media platforms. Think about it...

1. As said by Twitter expert Gary Loper in an interview I conducted with him, "Social media can connect people across town, to other cities, countries and continents. It spans across all socioeconomic and religious upbringings, ages and gender, professional and non-professional backgrounds; it reaches both personal and business levels."
2. Social media is great for connecting with veterans, veteran organizations, colleagues, recruiters, HR managers and experts in the fields.
3. Don't be overwhelmed with all the platforms out there. Choose what is right for you. LinkedIn is considered the platform for professionals, but if you have a large following on one platform, start there.

Using Social Media

- Search your name and see what is out there on you. Recruiters, hiring managers and potential business partners often do this and you want to avoid any surprises.
- Start making connections before you separate or retire. Look for colleagues, classmates, friends and family members you can connect with.
- Follow organizations that offer transition tips for the military such as MOAA (www.moaa.org).
- Get noticed and position yourself as an expert sharing short articles written by you and others.
- Include a photo – people are looking to connect with a person. Use one that is professional, not a shot of you taken in your bathroom mirror.
- Engage – like, share and comment to get noticed.
- Consider working with a Certified Social Media Career Strategist to get you started.

Step 9
LinkedIn

LinkedIn is the largest professional social media network in the world – and is where a large portion of transitioning military start. According to LinkedIn News Room, during the second quarter of 2016, LinkedIn had over 450 million members worldwide. I actually received one of the best job offers I ever got after retirement because someone looked at my LinkedIn profile and reached out to me.

1. To begin, set up a profile on at https://www.linkedin.com
2. Have only one profile.
3. Use your resume as a baseline to start your profile. Be sure to include volunteer work.
4. Your profile should represent the career field you desire to work in.
5. Conduct a search to see how many people share your name on LinkedIn. When I searched my name, I found 117 Carolyn Owens.

Additional Tips for LinkedIn:

- Look at other LinkedIn profiles in similar career fields and see how their profile is written. You can also take a look at my profile at: http://www.linkedin.com/in/cowensinfinitycoaching/
- When individuals look at your profile they are looking at shared connections, professional experience, number of connections, any writing published on LinkedIn, industry-related articles you have shared, cultural fit, and how you can possibly work together or help them.
- Engage with people. Do not send out a request blast, sending the same generic message to everyone.
- When connecting with someone, send them a personal message, not the standard one LinkedIn gives you to use - "I'd like to add you to my professional network on LinkedIn."
- This one bears repeating - DO include a picture! People want to see who they will be doing business with.

Step 10
Get a Mentor

A mentor is someone who has "been there and done that"; as such, they can serve as a role model. A mentor has a similar experience as the mentee and can show them the ropes. Ken Williams, author of *Mentoring the Next Generation of Non-Profit Leaders*, says, "Mentors can do a number of things for your career." Mentors can help you:

1. Build your resume.
2. Guide and/or assist you on a project.
3. Help you identify relevant resources.
4. Refer you to other mentors and important people in your field.
5. Share with you experiences and lessons learned.

Tips on Selecting the Right Mentor

- Find a mentor in the industry you are looking for. If you do not know the person you wish to be your mentor, begin by establishing a relationship with them. Follow them on social media; comment, like and share their posts.
- Choose someone you respect and meet with them first to make sure you are a good fit. Consider their position and workload, and don't take it personally if they say no.
- Know how you want to work with them. Will they help you with a specific skill? Will they give you advice on your career path? How will you meet and how often?
- Consider having more than one mentor. One could help you with a specific skill while another may provide career advice.
- Be a good mentee. Do not ask about their personal life unless they invite the conversation. Show up on time. Think of ways you can help them. Show your gratitude. Provide feedback on how what they have taught you or discussed with you has helped you.

Step 11
Writing Your Resume

Transform your resume into a POWERFUL self-marketing tool. Don't wait until the day before the transition class or just before you separate/retire to write your resume. While going through the transition assistance class, you will meet people who can take a moment to provide suggestions on how to improve your resume.

1. Gather your prior evaluations and awards and look to see if there is information you can use in your resume.
2. Focus on transferable skills that are applicable to any work setting, such as being organized or working as part of a team.
3. No one resume will fit each job. It must be updated to use the same language the employer uses and must reflect the criteria listed in the job announcement.
4. Have someone review your resume and provide feedback before you send it out. A second pair of eyes may catch spelling errors you might overlook. You may consider hiring a professional resume writer.
5. Your resume is your marketing tool – you must stand out and show your value!

A Few Points to Consider When Writing Your Resume:

- When writing your resume, keep in mind, the resume is what will get you the interview. The interview is what gets you the job.
- Don't write the resume for your current job, write it for the job you want.
- Make sure your resume is easy to read and write the resume in civilian terms, not military terms.
- Federal resumes and private sector resumes ARE NOT created equal (See Step 14).
- There are free, easy-to-use resume builders you can find online such as https://www.resume.com
- Five Steps to Rapid Employment is an excellent online program that teaches you how to stand out, write your resume and market yourself. Find out more about the program at: http://infinitycoaching.net/books-and-products.
- And, most importantly – Do Not Lie on Your Resume!

Step 12
The Roller Coaster Ride

The transition from military to civilian life can be a very frustrating and stressful time. If you are looking for a new job, it could take awhile depending on the time of year, geographic location, experience, salary requirements and age. During this time you can become angry, lose confidence, feel anxious and depressed, and even feel like a failure. Some people have become so frustrated with the process they lose their motivation and just want to give up. You must avoid destructive behavior such as alcohol, drug abuse or infidelity – as the consequences can be severe. To minimize the stress, negative feelings and emotions, identify what you can control and what you cannot.

1. Be committed and determined to have a successful transition and enjoy the process.
2. Have a positive attitude and learn how to control your emotions. A bad attitude can cause the process to last longer and you will most likely end up with a job you really don't want.
3. Consider working with a certified career coach to guide you through the process.

Here are Some Additional Tips to Help Manage the Process and Help You Remain Positive:

- Be disciplined – be aware of the amount of time and energy devoted to your transition and job search.
- Don't allow anyone else to control your emotions. There will be people who can influence your transition in a negative way by what they say to you, their thoughts, feelings and expectations of what you should not be doing. Surround yourself with positive people who support you.
- Continue an exercise regimen – many service members will gain a few extra pounds during the transition process.
- Take time to care of yourself. Go to a movie, spend time with friends and have fun. Remember – laughter is still the best medicine.
- Embrace failure and rejection. You may not get the first job you applied for and that's okay. Learn from the experience and think about what you can do differently.

Step 13
Compensation and Benefits

One of the most common things I hear is, I wish I had known more about how Veteran's Affairs compensation worked. Many veterans do not take time to fully understand the process before they are retired or separated. Some of the information is covered in the Transition Programs, but you may need to do a little research of your own.

1. Understand what your estimated retirement pay, separation pay or final paycheck will be, along with estimated taxes. Are you selling any leave back or are you taking terminal leave? For your financial plan, review and understand the tax free portions of your paycheck – housing allowance and BAS (Basic Allowance for Subsistence) . Your disbursing office can help you with this.
2. Know the timelines for filing your disability claim. The Benefits Delivery at Discharge (BDD) program allows a service member to submit a claim for disability compensation 60 to 180 days prior to separation, retirement or release from active duty or demobilization. BDD can help you receive VA disability benefits sooner, with a goal of within 60 days after release or discharge.

Resources You Should Review:

- The Quick Start program serves Service members who do not qualify for BDD because they have less than 60 days before separation/retirement and/or they are not able to make VA examinations at the point of separation.
- http://www.va.gov is the Department of Veterans Affairs website.
- On the VA website you can also find, The Federal Benefits for Veterans, Dependents and Survivors Handbook http://www.va.gov/opa/publications/benefits_book.asp
- Each State has information on the benefits they offer service members. Spend time researching and understanding what is offered.
- www.ebenefits.va.gov is an internet portal for Veterans, Service Members, their families and caregivers to access benefit-related tools and information. Set up your account before you retire or separate.
- Veteran Service Organizations are available to assist service members with understanding and filing for benefits and services. Select a VSO Representative, enter the zip code and/or state and you will receive a complete list. http://www.va.gov/ogc/apps/accreditation/index.asp

Step 14
Federal, Private or Non-Profit

In determining industries you want to work in, consider four primary routes you can take: Federal, Private Sector, Non-Profit or Entrepreneurship. Applying for a Federal job is different from private and non-profit sectors. Spend time exploring your options and decide which route aligns with your values, career and life goals.

For Federal Positions:

1. Familiarize yourself with the federal hiring process. Include how to target agencies, salaries, how the government hires, understand key terms, read and understand USAJOBS announcements. Having an understanding of the process will give you an edge. Consider attending a Federal Hiring Process workshop.
2. You can begin to apply for federal jobs 120 days before your separation/retirement date.
3. Mil2FedJobs www.mil2fedjobs.com is a great resource that anyone can use. It was created by the Maryland Department of Labor, Licensing and Regulations to translate military occupations to federal jobs, and more.

More Categories:

Private Sector:
- *5 Steps to Rapid Employment* book or online program, offers a step-by-step process for landing a job or making a successful career transition. To find out more about the online program, visit: http://infinitycoaching.net/books-and-products

Other Choices:
- Decide if you want to work for a non-profit or start your own.
- If you want to start your own, research courses you can take to educate yourself on the process. Gaining as much knowledge as you can first will avoid legal problems later.

Be Your Own Boss:
- Not finding the career you want? Consider striking out on your own.

Reference Books:
Military to Federal Career Guide, by Kathryn Troutman
Find Your Federal Job Fit, by Karol Taylor and Janet Ruck
E-Myth Revisited by Michael Gerber
5 Steps to Rapid Employment by Jay Block
The Go-Giver by Bob Burg and John David Mann

Step 15
Mindset

In the process of transitioning, there is also an emotional and mental piece that is part of the process and often overlooked. I have heard stories of those who did not adjust well and, as a result, took their own lives. When I talk to colleagues about their experience with the transition, here is some of the feedback I received:

1. "(You are) often put on a pedestal and told you are better than the rest of the private sector who have never served... The private sector is hiring you. (The) person you may have to interview with or work with may have never served and don't know your ranks, what it means... "
2. "I wish I had known more about the perception of former military members. I am so disappointed by the lack of leadership I see out here, and no one is surprised, but me...."
3. "Be nice to people, especially your new nonmilitary coworkers. They don't work for you, so you can't tell them what to do. Your "take charge" intimidates them. To successfully transition, you must remember nonmilitary folks think you are a bit strange."

Thoughts to Help Keep Things in Perspective and Positive:

As of November 2015, according to DMDC, only 7.3% of the U.S. population has ever served in the military. There is a large portion of the United States that has not experienced, nor do they fully understand, the military culture. The fact that you served stays with you, in your heart forever, but the uniform does not go with you in your next career.

- Things will not be as clear to you at times. Don't be afraid to ask questions.
- Be open to feedback, and don't take things personally. In some industries you may need to take an entry-level position to get into the career field.
- Respect those around you and be open to the perspective they are coming from.
- Study the culture of an organization and see where you can make a difference.
- Ask for help when needed, and in turn, help others who follow.
- Have a support system; talk to people who have been there, done that.

    Be proud of your service and welcome back to civilian life (CIVLANT)...

You've finished. Congratulations! You are now one step closer to a successful military transition. Before you go…

Tweet/share that you finished this book.

Please star rate this book.

Reviews are solid gold to writers. Please take a few minutes to give us some itty bitty feedback.

ABOUT THE AUTHOR

Carolyn R. Owens is a United States Navy veteran and the Chairwoman and CEO of Infinity Coaching, Inc., which provides career, leadership and life coaching that moves individuals forward, allowing them to take COMMAND of their lives. With over 25 years of proven experience, she is a leading authority on leadership and professional development and has worked with, and trained top leaders across the globe.

Having served in key leadership positions and as a successful business owner, she knows quite well some of the challenges one faces when pursuing the career and life of their dreams. Prior to starting her career at Infinity Coaching, Inc. Carolyn served in the United States Navy for over 24 years, retiring as a Navy Commander in 2012.

During her career, she has served as the director of Human Capital Management, an organization of over 4,800 civilians, military and contract personnel. Her favorite assignment while on active duty was when she served as a Professor in the Department of Command Leadership and Management at the United States Army War College. Upon retiring, she decided to turn the part she loved most about her job into a second career.

**If you enjoyed this Itty Bitty® Book
You might also enjoy…**

- **Your Amazing Itty Bitty® Safety Book** – Stephen C. Carpenter

- **Your Amazing Itty Bitty® Concussion Book** – Sheryl Hensel

- **Your Amazing Itty Bitty® Veteran's Survival Book** – Earl J. Katigbak

And many more Itty Bitty® Books available on the internet…

www.ingramcontent.com/pod-product-compliance
Lightning Source LLC
Chambersburg PA
CBHW061304040426
42444CB00010B/2514